THE BACKSLIDER

The Backslider

AN ENQUIRY INTO THE NATURE, SYMPTOMS,
AND EFFECTS OF RELIGIOUS DECLENSION,
WITH THE MEANS OF RECOVERY

BY

ANDREW FULLER

WITH AN INTRODUCTION BY THE
REV. JOHN ANGELL JAMES

I went by the field of the slothful, and by the vineyard of the man void of understanding; And, lo, it was all grown over with thorns, and nettles had covered the face thereof, and the stone wall thereof was broken down. Then I saw, and considered it well: I looked upon it, and received instruction.
—PROVERBS 24:30-32.

CURIOSMITH

MINNEAPOLIS

Published by Curiosmith.
Minneapolis, Minnesota.
Internet: curiosmith.com.

Previously published by WILLIAM BUTTON in 1801.

The "Guide to the Contents" was added to this edition by the publisher.

ISBN 9781941281727

GUIDE TO THE CONTENTS

INTRODUCTION

Andrew Fuller was, in my opinion, one of the greatest theologians, which modern times, or any times have produced, and his writings are an almost inexhaustible mine of doctrinal, practical, and experimental truth, which every Christian and especially every minister, would do well to explore. No man better understood the Bible, or the human heart both in its unrenewed and its regenerate state. Among all his various practical treatises, there are few, if any, of greater value than that on BACKSLIDING. Like a most skilful physician, he explains, with singular ability, the nature of the disease, lays down the symptoms of it, and prescribes the method of recovery.

Backsliding among professing Christians, if we include, as we ought to do, in this term, the secret departure of the heart from God, as well as the open sins of the life, is a state fearfully common. How many are there in all our churches, who give evidence, not to be doubted, of having lost "their first love." Before they were received into fellowship, the salvation of their soul seemed to be indeed the only one thing needful with them, and it was followed with a solicitude, diligence, and earnestness, that permitted none to question, their sincerity, or to hesitate on the propriety of admitting them to the church. For awhile they "ran well," and maintained their profession not only with external consistency, but as far as we could judge, with inward spirituality. Soon, however, the symptoms of declension were but too evident, in a diminished interest on the subject of religion, and in a less frequent attendance on its public ordinances, till at length nothing but the form of godliness remained, and even that so mutilated or wasted, as to have lost all its symmetry as well as its vitality. *This* is the kind of backsliding which is most prevalent, and against which the Christians of the present day of easy and unmolested profession, need to be cautioned. Immoralities rarely occur in comparison with the predominance of a worldly spirit. Many are going forward unobserved by others, perhaps scarcely suspected by themselves, in the backslider's path. Living in an age of commercial and political excitement, and acted upon by surrounding scenes, they have little time and less inclination for those exercises of devotion, self-examination, and watchfulness, which at all times are necessary, and especially so in the present, for maintaining or regaining the vitality of religion; and thus they slide down into a lukewarm state, and settle at length in a confirmed departure from God.

For such persons, as well as for those who have departed from God in life, as well as in heart, the treatise of Mr. Fuller is admirably adapted: it is faithful, searching, tender, and discriminating. The author handles his patient with a kind gentleness, yet probes the disease to the bottom; and with vigilant assiduity labors to restore him to sound health; carefully warning him, at the same time, against all deceptive indications of real cure.

Nor is it only for him who *is* a backslider that this treatise is designed, or valuable, but for him who *may become one*.

And who may not? "Let him that thinketh he standeth, take heed lest he fall."[1] They who are going, or are gone back, appeared once to be advancing. We live in a world of trials; and temptation, like the wind, comes to all, and from every quarter. The way not to backslide, is to be afraid of it. Self-confidence has proved, in innumerable cases, to be the fore-runner of self-destruction. This little work may be read by all professors with great advantage, if perused in a spirit of prayer and holy jealousy. I am well pleased that it is republished in a separate form; most cordially recommend it, and shall be happy to know it has obtained a wide circulation.

J. A. JAMES

Edgbaston, near Birmingham,
July, 1840.

---

1 1 Corinthians 10:12.

AUTHOR'S PREFACE

The following pages were occasioned by the writer's observing several persons of whom he had formerly entertained a favorable opinion, and with whom he had walked in Christian fellowship, having fallen, either from the doctrine, or practice of pure religion. A view of their unhappy condition made a deep impression upon his mind. If he has been enabled to describe the case of a backslider to any good purpose, it has been chiefly owing to this circumstance. He hopes that, though it was written with a special eye to a few, it may yet be useful to many.

AUTHOR'S INTRODUCTION

Whether the present age be worse than others which have preceded it, I shall not determine; but this is manifest, that it abounds not only in infidelity and profligacy, but with great numbers of loose characters among professing Christians. It is true there are some eminently zealous and spiritual, perhaps as much so as at almost any former period; the disinterested concern which has appeared for the diffusion of evangelical religion is doubtless a hopeful feature of our times: yet it is no less evident that others are in a sad degree conformed to this world, instead of being transformed by the renewing of their minds. Even of those who retain a decency of character, many are sunk into a Laodicean lukewarmness. Professors are continually falling away from Christ; either totally, so as to walk no more with him, or partially, so as greatly to dishonor his name. Alas, how many characters of this description are to be found in our congregations! If we only review the progress of things for twenty or thirty years past, we shall perceive many who once bid fair for the kingdom of heaven, now fallen a prey to the temptations of the world. Like the blossoms of the spring, they for a time excited our hopes: but a blight has succeeded: the blossom *has gone up as the dust*, and *the root* in many cases appears to be *rottenness*.[1]

It is one important branch of the work of a faithful pastor to strengthen the diseased, to heal the sick, to bind up the broken, to bring again that which is driven away, and to seek that which is lost.[2] If these pages shall fall into the hands of but a few of the above description, and contribute in any degree to their recovery from the snare of the devil, the writer will be amply rewarded. It is a pleasure to recover any sinner from the error of his way; but much more those of whom we once thought favorably. The place which they formerly occupied in our esteem, our hopes, and our social exercises, now seems to be a kind of chasm, which can only be filled up by their return to God. If a child depart from his father's house, and plunge into profligacy and ruin, the father may have other children, and may love them; but none of them can heal his wound, nor anything satisfy him, but the return of *him who was lost.*

In pursuit of this desirable object, I shall describe the nature and different species of backsliding from God—notice the symptoms of it—trace its injurious and dangerous effects—and point out the means of recovery.

---

1 See Isaiah 5:24.
2 See Ezekiel 34:4.

Chapter 1

ON THE GENERAL NATURE AND DIFFERENT SPECIES OF BACKSLIDING

All backsliding from God originates in a departure of heart from him: herein consists the essence and the evil of it. *Thine own wickedness shall correct thee, and thy backslidings shall reprove thee: know therefore and see that it is an evil thing and bitter, that* THOU HAST FORSAKEN THE LORD THY GOD, *and that my fear is not in thee, saith the Lord GOD of hosts.*[1] But the degrees of this sin, and the modes in which it operates, are various.

The backsliding of some is TOTAL.—After having made a profession of the true religion, they apostatize from it. I am aware it is common to consider a backslider as being a good man, though in a bad state of mind: but the scriptures do not confine the term to this application. Those who are addressed in the passage just quoted, had not *the fear of God in them,* which can never be said of a good man. Backsliding, it is true, always supposes a *profession* of the true religion: but it does not necessarily suppose the existence of the thing professed. There is a PERPETUAL *backsliding,* and a *drawing back* UNTO PERDITION.[2] Such characters were Saul, and Ahithophel, and Judas.

1 Jeremiah 2:19.
2 Jeremiah 8:5; Hebrews 10:39.

Many persons who have in a great degree declined the practice
of religion, yet comfort themselves with an idea that they shall
be brought to repentance before they die; but this is presump-
tuously tempting God. Whosoever plunges in this gulf, or continues easy in it, under an idea of being recovered by repentance, may find himself mistaken. Both Peter and Judas went
in; but only one of them came out! There is reason to fear that
thousands of professors are now lifting up their eyes in torment,
who in this world reckoned themselves good men; who considered their sins as pardonable errors, and laid their accounts
with being brought to repentance: but ere they were aware,
the bridegroom came, and they were not ready to meet him!

The nature and deadly tendency of sin is the same in
itself, whether in a wicked or in a righteous man: there is an
important difference, however, between the backsliding of the
one, and that of the other. That of the hypocrite arises from
his having *no root* in himself: therefore it is that in time of
temptation he falleth away: but that of the sincere Christian
respects the culture of the branch, and is owing to unwatchful-
ness or remissness in duty. The first, in turning back, returns
to a course which his heart always preferred: the last, though in
what he does he is not absolutely involuntary, for then it were
innocent: yet it is not with a full or perfect consent of will. He
does not sin *wilfully:* that which he does he *allows not:* it is
against the *habitual disposition* of his soul: he is not himself, as
we should say, while so acting.[1] Finally, the one, were it not for

---

1 It is usual to denominate a character by his habitual or ruling disposition,
and not by occasional deviations from it. Thus, when we hear of him who was
famed for *meekness*, speaking *unadvisedly* with his lips, we say this was not
Moses; or of him who was distinguished for his courageous avowal of his Lord,
denying with oaths that he knew him, we say this was not Peter. Both these
great characters in these instances acted *beside themselves;* it was not *them*, as
it were, but sin that dwelt in them. See Hebrews 10:26; Romans 7:15–25.

the remorse of conscience which may continue to haunt him, and disturb his peace, would be in his element in having made a full riddance of religion: but this is not the case with the other. A life of deviation and distance from God is not his element, nor can he enjoy himself in it. This difference is remarkably exemplified in the cases of Saul and David. The religion of the former never appears to have fitted him: he was continually acting awkwardly with it, and presently threw it aside. If, in addition to this, he could have forgotten it, and lived without being terrified by the apprehension of consequences, he would doubtless have been much the happier for having cast it off. But when the latter had sinned, he was not like the raven which went forth of the ark, and came no more: but like the dove which could find no rest for the sole of her foot till she returned. The thirty-second and thirty-eighth psalms express the wretchedness of his mind till he confessed his sin, and obtained mercy.

But whatever difference there be between a partial and a total departure from God, it will be difficult, if not impossible, for the person himself at the time to perceive it. So long as any man continues in a backsliding state, the reality of his religion must remain uncertain. He may not be without hope, nor ought he to be without fear. The scriptures know nothing of that kind of confidence which renders men easy in their sins. Paul stood in *doubt* of the Galatians, and they ought to have stood in doubt of themselves.—The species of backsliding are various: some respect doctrine, others practice; but all are the operations of a heart departing from the living God.

In some a backsliding spirit first appears BY A RELINQUISHMENT OF EVANGELICAL DOCTRINE—Where truth is treated as a matter of speculation, or as an opinion of no great moment, it is not *held fast;* and where this is the case, it is easily surrendered. If a plausible book, in favor of deism, or any of those vain systems which nearly approach it, fall in their way, they are ready to yield; and by reading the performance a second time, or conversing with a person who favors it, they make shipwreck of their faith, and are driven on the rocks of infidelity. Such was the process in the days of the apostles; those who received not the *love of the truth*, were given up to *believe a lie*.[1]

If these departures from evangelical principles were closely examined, it would be found that they were preceded by a neglect of private prayer, watchfulness, self-diffidence, and walking humbly with God; and every one may perceive that they are followed with similar effects. It has been acknowledged by some who have embraced the Socinian system, that since they entertained those views they had lost even the gift of prayer. Perhaps they might draw up and read an *address to the Deity;* but they could not pray. Where the principles of the gospel are abandoned, the spirit of prayer, and of all close walking with God, will go with it. The confession of Peter, that *Jesus was the Christ, the Son of God*, is thought to be that which our Lord denominates the *rock* on which he would build his church. We are sure that the belief of this article of faith was required as a kind of test of Christianity; and who can look into the Christian world with attention, and not perceive that it still continues a sort of key-stone to the building? If this give way, the fabric falls. Backslidings of this nature are infinitely dangerous. He that declines in holy practice has to labor against the remonstrances of conscience: but he that brings himself to think lightly of sin, and meanly of the Saviour (which is what every false system of religion teaches) has gone far towards silencing the accusations of this

1 2 Thessalonians 2:10, 11.

unpleasant monitor. He is upon good terms with himself. The disorder of his soul is deep; but it is of a flattering nature. The declension of serious religion in him is no less apparent to *others*, than that of the constitution by a consuming hectic; yet, as is common in such cases, the person himself thinks he shall do well. In short, the *light which is in them is darkness;* and this is the greatest of all darkness!

In others a departure of heart from God is followed by FALLING INTO SOME GROSS IMMORALITY.—There are instances in which a sudden misconduct of this sort has been overruled for the awakening of the mind from its stupor, and divesting it of its self-confidence. It was manifestly thus with the apostle Peter. The stumbling of such persons is not that they should fall; but rather that they should stand with greater care and firmness. But the greatest danger arises from those cases where some lust of the flesh has gradually obtained an ascendancy over the heart; so that when the subject of it falls in the eyes of the world, it is only appearing to be what he has long been in secret; and the first wrong step that he makes, instead of alarming him, and occasioning his going aside to weep bitterly, is only the prelude of a succession of others. This is not the fall of one who is *overtaken* in a fault; but of one who is entangled in the net of his own corruptions. One sin prepares the way for another. Like the insect infolded in the spider's web, he loses all power of resistance, and falls a prey to the destroyer. Some have fallen sacrifices to intemperance, not by being overtaken in a single act of intoxication; but by contracting a habit of hard drinking. First, it was indulged in private, perhaps under some outward trouble, instead of carrying it to a throne of grace. In a little time its demands increased. At length, it could no longer be kept a secret: reason was enslaved to sense, and the Christian professor sunk below the man! Others have indulged in impurity. Intimacies which may have arisen from nothing worse than a few improper familiarities; yea, which in some instances have originated in religion itself, through the corrupt propensities of the human heart, which turns everything it touches into poison, have been known to produce the most fatal effects. Passions of this sort once kindled will soon possess all the soul. They leave no room for anything that should resist them: not only consuming every spiritual desire and holy thought, but banishing from the mind even the sober dictates of reason; reducing the most exalted characters to the rank of *fools in Israel*. Near these rocks are seen many a floating wreck; and among these quicksands numbers, who once bid fair for the haven of everlasting life.

Another way in which a departure from God very often operates, is, by THE LOVE OF THIS WORLD.—It is not uncommon for persons who once appeared to be zealous, affectionate, and devoted to God, when they come to be settled in life, and to enter into its necessary avocations, to lose all heart for religion, and take no delight in any thing but saving money. This, it is true, is not generally considered by the world as disreputable: on the contrary, provided we be fair in our dealings, it is reckoned a mark of wisdom. *Men will praise thee when thou doest well for thyself.*[1] Such a one, say they, is a discreet man, and one that knows how to secure the *main chance*. Yet the scriptures are very decisive against such characters. This is the sin which they denominate the *lust of the eye*.[2] The cares, and riches, and pleasures of this life, are described as *choking the Word*, and rendering it unfruitful. It is worthy of special notice, that when our Lord had warned his followers *to take heed and beware of covetousness*, the example which he gives

1 Psalm 49:18.
2 1 John 2:16.

of this sin, is not of one that was a plunderer of other men's property, an unfair dealer, or an oppressor of the poor; but of a *certain rich man whose ground brought forth plentifully;* and whose only object appeared to be, first to acquire a handsome fortune, and then to retire from business and live at his ease.[1] This also appears to be the character which is *blessed* by wicked men but *abhorred of God.*[2] A man who deals unfairly with men, gains not their blessing, but their curse. Men in general regard only themselves: so long, therefore, as any person deals justly with them, they care not what his conduct is towards God. But it is affecting to think, that the very character which they bless and envy, God abhors. The decision of heaven is nothing less than this, *If any man love the world, the love of the Father is not in him?*[3] So far is the love of the world from being the less dangerous on account of its falling so little under human censure, that it is the more so. If we be guilty of anything which exposes us to the reproach of mankind, such reproach may assist the remonstrances of conscience, and of God, in carrying conviction to our bosoms; but of that for which the world acquits us, we shall be exceedingly disposed to acquit ourselves.

It has long appeared to me that this species of covetousness will, in all probability, prove the eternal overthrow of more characters among professing people, than almost any other sin; and this because it is almost the only sin which may be indulged, and a profession of religion at the same time supported. If a man be a drunkard, a fornicator, an adulterer, or a liar; if he rob his neighbor, oppress the poor, or deal unjustly, he must give up his pretences to religion; or if not, his religious

---

1 Luke 12:15–21.
2 Psalm 10:3.
3 1 John 2:15.

connections, if they are worthy of being so denominated, will give him up: but he may *love the world, and the things of the world*, and at the same time retain his character. If the depravity of the human heart be not subdued by the grace of God, it will operate. If a dam be placed across some of its ordinary channels, it will flow with greater depth and rapidity in those which remain. It is thus, perhaps, that avarice is most prevalent in old age, when the power of pursuing other vices has in a great measure subsided. And thus it is with religious professors whose hearts are not right with God. They cannot figure away with the profane, or indulge in gross immoralities: but they can love the world supremely, to the neglect of God, and be scarcely amenable to human judgment.

And whatever may prove the overthrow of a mere professor, may be a temptation to a good man, and greatly injure his soul. Of this the case of *Lot*, when he parted with Abraham, furnishes an affecting example. When a situation was put to his choice, *he lifted up his eyes and beheld the plain of Jordan, that it was well watered everywhere;*[1] and he took up his residence in Sodom. He had better have dwelt in a wilderness, than among that debauched people: but he consulted worldly advantages, and the spiritual well-being of his family was overlooked. And what was the consequence? It is true, he was a righteous man, and his righteous soul was grieved with the filthy conversation of the wicked from day to day: but he could have very little influence over them, while they, on the contrary, found means of communicating their odious vices to his family. Some of his daughters appear to have been married while in Sodom, and when the city was to be destroyed, neither they nor their husbands could be persuaded to make their escape, and so probably perished in the overthrow. The heart of his

1 Genesis 13:10.

wife was so attached, it seems, to what she had left behind, that she must needs *look back;* for which she was rendered a monument of divine displeasure. And as to his two single daughters, though they had escaped with him to the mountain, yet they had learnt so much the ways of Sodom, as to cover his old age with infamy. This, together with the loss of all his substance, were the fruits of the *well-watered plain,* which he had fixed his eyes upon, to the neglect of his spiritual interest. Yet how frequently is the same part acted over again. In the choice of settlements for ourselves, or our children, how common is it to overlook the immorality of the place, the irreligiousness of the connections, and the want of a gospel ministry; and to direct our inquiries only to temporal advantages. From the same principle also many have dealt largely in speculation, and plunged into engagements far beyond their circumstances. The hope of making a fortune, as it is termed, by some lucky hit, draws them into measures which ruin not only themselves, but many that confide in them. That mere worldly men should act in this manner, is not a matter of surprise; but that men professing to fear God should imitate them—*this is a lamentation, and shall be for a lamentation.*

Farther, many have fallen sacrifices not only to the love of the world, but to a CONFORMITY TO IT.—These are not the same thing, though frequently found in the same person. The object of the one is principally the acquisition of wealth; the other respects the manner of spending it. That is often penurious; this wishes to cut a figure, and to appear like people of fashion. The former is *the lust of the eye;* the latter is *the pride of life.* We used not affect singularity in things indifferent; but to engage in the chase of fashionable appearance, is not only an indication of a vain and little mind, but is certainly inconsistent with pressing towards the mark, for the prize of the high calling of God in Christ Jesus. The desire of making an appearance, has ruined many people in their circumstances, more in their characters, and most in their souls. We may flatter ourselves that we can pursue these things, and be religious at the same time; but it is a mistake. The vanity of mind which they cherish, eats up everything of a humble, serious, and holy nature; rendering us an easy prey to temptation when solicited to do as others do in an evil thing. A Christian's rule is the revealed will of God: and where the customs of the world run counter to this, it is his business to withstand them, even though in so doing he may have to withstand a multitude, yea, and a multitude of people of fashion; but if we feel ambitious of their applause we shall not be able to endure the scorn which a singularity of conduct will draw upon us. Thus we shall be carried down the stream by the course of this world; and shall either fall into the gulf of perdition, or if any good should be found in us towards the Lord God of Israel, it will be almost indiscernible and useless. In short, such characters are certainly in a backsliding state, whether they be ever recovered from it or not. The case of the Laodiceans seems to approach the nearest to theirs of anything which in Scripture occurs to me. They were *neither cold nor hot;* neither the decided friends of Christ, nor his avowed enemies: they could not relinquish the world in favor of religion, yet neither could they let religion alone. They were vainly puffed up with a notion of their wealth, their wisdom, and their finery; saying, *I am rich, and increased in goods, and have need of nothing;* but in the account of the faithful and true Witness they were *poor, and blind, and wretched, and miserable, and naked.* Such a decision ought to make us tremble at the thought of aspiring to imitate people of fashion.

Finally, there is another species of departure from God,

which it becomes me to notice, as many in the present age have fallen sacrifices to it. This is, TAKING AN EAGER AND DEEP INTEREST IN POLITICAL DISPUTES.—The state of things in the world has of late been such as to attract the attention, and employ the conversation, of all classes of people. As success has attended each of the contending parties, the minds of men, according to their views and attachments, have been affected; some with fear and dismay lest their party interests should be ruined; others with the most sanguine hopes, as if the world were shortly to be emancipated, war abolished, and all degrees of men rendered happy. This is one of those strong winds of temptation that occasionally arise in the troubled ocean of this world, against which those who are bound to a better had need be on their guard. The flattering objects held out by revolutionists were so congenial with the wishes of humanity, and their pretences to disinterested philanthropy so fair, that many religious people, for a time, forgot their own principles. While gazing on the splendid spectacle, it did not occur to them that *the wicked*, whatever name they assumed, *would do wickedly*. By observing the progress of things however, they have been convinced that all hopes of the state of mankind being essentially meliorated by any means short of the prevalence of the gospel, are visionary, and have accordingly turned their attention to better things. But some have gone greater lengths. Their whole heart has been engaged in this pursuit. It has been their meat and their drink: and this being the case, it is not surprising that they have become indifferent to religion; for these things cannot consist with each other. It is not only contrary to the whole tenor of the New Testament, but tends in its own nature to eat up true religion. If any worldly matter, however lawful in itself, engage our attention inordinately, it becomes a snare; and more so in matters that do not come within the line of our immediate duty. But if in attending to it we neglect what manifestly *is* our duty, and overleap the boundaries of God's Holy Word, let us look to it: beyond those boundaries is a pit, in which, there is reason to fear, great numbers have been lost. There were many in the early age of Christianity who *despised government*, and were not afraid to speak evil of dignities: but were they good men? Far from it. They were professors of Christianity, however; for they are said to have *escaped the pollutions of the world, through the knowledge of Christ;* yea, and what is more, they had attained the character of Christian *teachers.* But of what description? *False teachers, who privily brought in damnable heresies, denying the Lord who bought them, bringing upon themselves swift destruction*—whose *ways*, though *followed by many,* were *pernicious*, occasioning *the way of truth to be evil spoken of.*[1] To copy the examples of such men is no light matter.

When a man's thoughts and affections are filled with such things as these, the scriptures become a kind of *dead letter*, while the speeches and writings of politicians are the *lively oracles:* spiritual conversation is unheard, or if introduced by others, considered as a flat and uninteresting topic; and leisure hours, whether sitting in the house or walking by the way, instead of being employed in talking and meditating on divine subjects, are engrossed by things which do not profit. Such are the rocks amongst which many have made shipwreck of their faith and a good conscience.

Whatever may be the duty of a nation in extraordinary cases, there is scarcely any thing in all the New Testament inculcated with more solemnity, than that individuals, and especially Christians, should be obedient, peaceable, and loyal subjects: nor is there any sin much more awfully censured than

1 2 Peter 2:1, 2.

the contrary conduct. It requires not only that we keep within the compass of the laws, (which is easily done by men of the most unprincipled minds) but that we honor, and *intercede with God* for those who administer them. These duties were pressed particularly upon the Romans, who, by their situation, were more exposed than others to the temptation of joining in factions and conspiracies, which were almost continually at work in that tumultuous city.

Nor does the danger belong exclusively to one side. We may sin by an adherence to the measures of a government, as well as by an opposition to them. If we enlist under the banners of the party in power, *considered as a party*, we shall feel disposed to vindicate or palliate all their proceedings, which may be very inconsistent with Christianity. Paul, though he enjoined obedience to the existing government, yet was never an advocate for Roman ambition; and when addressing himself to a governor, did not fail *to reason on righteousness, temperance, and judgment to come.* It is our duty, no doubt, to consider that many things which seem evil to us might appear otherwise, if all the circumstances of the case were known, and therefore to forbear passing hasty censures: but on the other hand, we ought to beware of applauding every thing that is done, lest, if it be evil, we be partakers of other men's sins, and contribute to their being repeated.

While some, burning with revolutionary zeal, have imagined they could discover all the wonderful events of the present day in scripture prophecy, and have been nearly blinded to the criminality of the principal agents, others, by a contrary prejudice, have disregarded the works of the Lord, and the operations of his hand. Whatever may be said of means and instruments, we must be strangely insensible not to see the hand of God in the late overturnings among the papal powers;

and if we be induced by political attachment, instead of joining the inhabitants of heaven in a song of praise, to unite with
the *merchants of the earth* in their lamentations, are we not
carnal? There is no need of vindicating or palliating the measures of men which may be wicked in the extreme: but neither
ought we to overlook the hand of God.

The great point with Christians should be, an attachment
to government, *as government*, irrespective of the party which
administers it; for this is right, and would tend more than anything to promote the kingdom of Christ. We are not called to
yield up our consciences in religious matters; nor to approve of
what is wrong in those which are civil; but we are not at liberty
to deal in acrimony, or evil speaking. The good which results
to society from the very worst government upon earth, is great
when compared with the evils of anarchy. On this principle, it
is probable, the apostle enjoined obedience *to the powers that
were*, even during the reign of Nero. Christians are soldiers
under the King of Kings: their object should be to conquer all
ranks and degrees of men to the obedience of faith. But to do
this, it is necessary that they avoid all those entanglements and
disputes which retard their main design. If a wise man wishes
to gain over a nation to any great and worthy object, he does
not enter into their little differences, nor embroil himself in
their party contentions; but bearing good will to all, seeks the
general good; by these means he is respected by all, and all are
ready to hear what he has to offer. Such should be the wisdom of Christians. There is enmity enough for us to encounter
without unnecessarily adding to it.

If a Christian be under the necessity of siding with a party,
undoubtedly he ought to be in favor of that which appears to
him the best: but even in this case it is not becoming him to
enter with eagerness into their disputes. Let worldly men, who

thirst after preferment, busy themselves in a contested elec-
tion—they have their reward—but let Christians, if called to
appear, discharge their duty, and retire from the tumultuous
scene.

By entering deeply into the *party* contentions of the
nation, religious people on both sides will be charged in their
turn with disloyalty; and it may be not always without a cause.
Fifty years ago, that party was out of power which at present
is in power. At that time the charge of disloyalty was directed
against them; and they were then denominated *patriots*. It is
possible, that many who now seem to abhor a spirit of disaffec-
tion towards administrative government, would be themselves
not the best affected, were the other side to recover its author-
ity. But if we enter into the spirit of the gospel, though we may
have our preferences of men and measures, we shall bear good-
will to all, and whoever be at the head of affairs, shall reverence
the powers that be. Whatever be our private opinion of the
men, we shall respect and honor the rulers. That loyalty which
operates only with the prevalence of a party, whichever it be, is
at a great remove from the loyalty enjoined by the scriptures.

By standing aloof from all parties *as such*, and approv-
ing themselves the friends of government and good order, by
whomsoever administered, Christians would acquire a dignity
of character worthy of their profession, would be respected by
all, and possess greater opportunities of doing good: while by a
contrary conduct they render one part of the community their
enemies, and the other, I fear, derive but little spiritual advantage from being their friends.

Chapter 2

ON THE SYMPTOMS OF A
BACKSLIDING SPIRIT

I t was reckoned a matter of consequence in cases of leprosy, real or supposed, that the true state of the person should be examined, and judgment given accordingly;[1] and by how much a moral disease is more odious, contagious, and dangerous than one that is natural, by so much is it more necessary to form a true judgment concerning it. Every spot was not a leprosy; and every sinful imperfection in a Christian professor does not denominate him a backslider. Paul had to lament the *body of death;* he had not attained, nor was he already perfect; yet he *pressed forward;* and while this was the case he could not be said to draw back. On the other hand, every departure from God must not be reckoned a mere imperfection which is common to good men. We are extremely apt, in certain cases, to flatter ourselves that our spots are only the spots of God's children, or such as the best of men are subject to, and therefore to conclude that there is nothing very dangerous about them. We do not pretend to deny that we have our faults: but are ready to ask, *What have we done* so MUCH *against thee?* This self-justifying spirit, however, so far from indicating anything favorable, is a strong mark of the

1 Leviticus 13.

contrary. It is said of Ephraim, *He is a merchant, the balances of deceit are in his hand: he loveth to oppress. And Ephraim said, Yet I am become rich: I have found me out substance: In all my labors they shall find none iniquity in me that were sin.*[1] A more finished picture of a modern oppressor could not be drawn. He studies to keep within the limits of the law, and defies any man to impeach his character: he has imperfections, but they are only such as are common to good men: there is nothing criminal to be found in him: yet he is carrying on at the time a system of iniquity.

The apostle Paul speaks of a certain state of mind which he feared he should find in the Corinthians; that of their *having sinned, and not repented of their deeds.* This it is which denominates a man a backslider; and which, so long as it continues, deprives him of any scriptural foundation for concluding himself interested in forgiving mercy.—What are the particular symptoms of this state of mind, is the object of our present inquiry.

If our departing from the Lord have issued in some outward misconduct, there is no need of inquiring into the proofs of it, as the thing speaks for itself; but if its operations have been at present only internal, the inquiry may be highly necessary, that we may become acquainted with our condition, and that the disease may be healed ere it finishes its operations. Further, though it may be out of all doubt that we have sinned, yet it may be a matter of uncertainty, whether we have, or have not repented; if we imagine we have when we have not, the consequence may be of the most serious nature. Let the following observations then be attended to.

First, IF RELIGIOUS DUTIES ARE ATTENDED TO RATHER FROM CUSTOM OR CONSCIENCE THAN LOVE, we must either

1 Hosea 12:7, 8.

never have known what true religion is, or in a great degree have lost the spirit of it.—It is possible that we may have been guilty of no particular outward evil, so as to have fallen under the censure of the world, or even our nearest connections; and yet have so far lost the spirit of religion as to be really in a backsliding state. The exercises of prayer, reading the scriptures, hearing the Word, and giving something to the poor, may be kept up in form, and yet be little or anything more than a form. The church of Ephesus was not accused of any particular outward misconduct; but they had *left their first love*. Where this is the case, however, much will be neglected, especially of those parts of duty which fall not under the eye of creatures. It is supposed of the church just referred to, that they had relaxed, if not in the actual performance, yet in the manner of performing their religious exercises; therefore they are exhorted to *repent and to do their first works*. A departure from our first love is commonly the first step of a backsliding course. Perhaps if the truth were known, there are few open falls but what are preceded by a secret departure of heart from the living God.

Secondly, IF WE HAVE FALLEN INTO ANY PARTICULAR SIN, WHICH EXPOSES US TO THE CENSURES OF OUR FRIENDS, AND INSTEAD OF CONFESSING IT WITH SORROW, ARE EMPLOYED IN DEFENDING OR PALLIATING IT, it is a certain proof that we are at present under the power of it.—There are some sins that cannot be defended; but there are others which will admit of much to be said on their behalf; and it is admirable with what ingenuity men will go about to find excuses where self is concerned. People that you would think hardly possessed of common sense, will in this case be singularly quick-sighted, discerning every circumstance that may make in their favor, or serve to extenuate their fault. The cunning of the old serpent which appeared in the excuses of our first parents, seems here to supply the place of wisdom.—This self-justifying spirit is a very dangerous symptom: while it continues there is no hope of a good issue. We read of the *deceitfulness* of sin: and truly it is with great propriety that deceit is ascribed to it. Perhaps there are few persons who are employed in justifying their failings, but who are first imposed upon, or brought to think, somehow, that they are, if not quite justifiable, yet very excusable. Sin, when *we* have committed it, loses its sinfulness, and appears a very different thing from what it did in others. David's indignation could rise against the man that had taken an ewe-lamb, while to his own conduct, which was much more criminal, he was blinded! When any sin is committed by *us,* it is common for it to assume *another name;* and by means of this we become easily reconciled to it, and we are ready to enter on a vindication of it. Covetousness will admit of a defense under the names of prudence, industry, or frugality: conformity to the world may be pleaded for as an exercise of sociability and good breeding; unchristian resentment as necessary self-defense; foolish levity as innocent mirth; malignant contentions as zeal for the truth; and indifference to the truth as candor, or liberality of sentiment.

Thirdly, THOUGH WE DO NOT DEFEND OR PALLIATE OUR SIN IN WORDS, YET IF WE CONTINUE IN THE PRACTICE OF IT, we may be certain we have not repented.—All true repentance is followed by a *forsaking* of the evil, and where this effect is not produced, there can be no scriptural ground to hope for forgiveness. There are sins as before observed, which will admit of no defense. If a person be convicted of them, he can do no other than own himself in the wrong, or at least be silent: yet he may feel no sorrow on their account, nor scarcely any intention to forsake them. When Samuel reproved Saul for his rebellion against the commandment of the Lord, assuring him that God had rejected him from being King, and had given the kingdom to a neighbor of his that was better than he, he was confounded, and compelled to say, *I have sinned:* yet the only concern he discovered was on account of having lost his *honor;* and as soon as he suspected who was his rival, he sought to slay him. Even Solomon discovered a very similar disposition. Instead of lamenting and forsaking the sin for which he had been reproved, as soon as he knew that Jeroboam had been anointed by the prophet Ahijah, he *sought to kill him.*[1] A sullen silence under reproof, and a perseverance in the evil, are certain signs of a hard and impenitent heart.

Fourthly, THOUGH WE SHOULD REFRAIN FROM THE PRACTICE OF THE EVIL, YET IF IT BE ONLY A TEMPORARY EFFECT OF CONVICTION, there is no true repentance. It is very common for persons when they fall into any gross sin to feel ashamed and alarmed, to wish they had not acted as they have, and to resolve that they will do so no more: and this, though the love of the evil be the same, and on the first temptation that returns it is committed again, is nevertheless frequently mistaken for repentance. When Saul's life was spared by David, and his groundless malice against him was detected, his heart seemed to relent; he felt ashamed, owned his sin, lifted up his voice and wept, and promised to do so no more; but this was not repentance. David appears to have suspected it at the time; for he would not trust himself in his hands; but gat him up into the hold:[2] and the event justified his conduct. The first opportunity that offered, Saul returned to the folly he had condemned.—A temporary abstinence from evil may soon be produced by some *alarming providence.* When judgments

1 1 Samuel 15; 1 Kings 11.
2 1 Samuel 24.

overtake us, and conscience tells us that it is the hand of the Lord stretched out against us for our sin, the mind is appalled with fear, and so ceases to be in a state to pursue its favorite devices. But if as soon as the pressing hand of providence is removed, the heart returns like a spring, to its former position, there is no reason to consider its temporary depression as containing any true repentance.

Dr. OWEN has expressed these sentiments with that unction of spirit, and deep insight into the human heart which is peculiar to himself.—

"There are two occasions, says he, wherein men who are contending with any sin, may seem to themselves to have mortified it.—First, when it hath had some sad eruption to the disturbance of their peace, terror of their consciences, dread of scandal, and evident provocation of God. This awakens and stirs up all that is in the man and amazes him, fills him with abhorrency of sin, and himself for it; sends him to God, makes him cry out as for life, to abhor his lust as hell, and to set himself against it. The whole man spiritual and natural, being now awakened, sin shrinks in its head, appears not, but lies as dead before him. As when one that hath drawn nigh to an army in the night, and hath killed a principal person; instantly the guards awake, men are roused up, and strict inquiry is made after the enemy; who in the mean time, until the noise and tumult be over, hides himself or lies like one that is dead, yet with firm resolution to do the like mischief again upon the like opportunity.—Secondly, in a time of some judgment, calamity, or pressing affliction. The heart is then taken up with thoughts and contrivances of flying from the present troubles, fears, and dangers. This, as a convinced person concludes, is to be done only by relinquishment of sin, which gains peace with God. It is the anger of God in every affliction that galls a convinced person. To be quit of this, men resolve at such times against their sins. Sin shall never more have any place in them; they will never again give themselves up to the service of it. Accordingly sin is quiet, stirs not, seems to be mortified: not indeed that it has received any one wound, but merely because the soul hath possessed its faculties whereby it should exert itself, with thoughts inconsistent with the motions thereof; which when they are laid aside, sin returns again to its former life and vigor. Of this we have a full instance in Psalm 78:32–38. *For all this they sinned still, and believed not for his wondrous works. Therefore their days did he consume in vanity, and their years in trouble. When he slew them, then they sought him: and they returned and enquired early after God. And they remembered that God was their rock, and the high God their redeemer. Nevertheless they did flatter him with their mouth, and they lied unto him with their tongues. For their heart was not right with him, neither were they steadfast in his covenant.* I no way doubt but when they sought and returned, and enquired earnestly after God, they did it with full purpose of heart, as to the relinquishment of their sins. This is expressed in the word *returned*. To *turn*, or *return* unto the Lord is by a relinquishment of sin. And this they did *early*, with earnestness and diligence; but yet their sin was unmodified for all this, verses 36, 37: and this is the state of many humiliations in the days of affliction, and a great deceit in the hearts of believers themselves, lies oftentimes herein."[1]

When a professor of religion has fallen into drunkenness, uncleanness, or some such odious vice, and wishes to shelter himself from the censures of his connections, you will often hear him allege "I have *repented*": whereas it amounts to little more than the shame and alarm above described, as his after

1 *Of the Mortification of Sin in Believers* by John Owen, chapter 5.

conduct very frequently proves. Indeed, it is not of the nature of true repentance to talk of *having* repented, and especially for the purpose of evading a faithful censure.

Fifthly, THOUGH WE SHOULD REFRAIN FROM THE OPEN PRACTICE OF THE SIN, AND THAT FOR A CONTINUANCE; YET IF IT BE MERELY FROM PRUDENTIAL OR SELFISH CONSIDERATIONS, we may be certain that we have not yet repented of it.—Though we had no religion and pretended to none, we might find various inducements to refrain from gross immoralities. They affect our interest, our health, our reputation: it is on such principles that mere worldly men will guard against them; and if we act from the same motives, wherein are we better than they? Or if the dread of future punishment may be supposed to have some influence upon us, this is a very different thing from the fear of the Lord, which is to *hate* evil. And where the motives for abstaining from any evil are merely prudential, or selfish, we shall abstain from very little more than that which falls under the eye of creatures. Our watchfulness will respect little, if anything, more than outward actions. The daily care of our lives will be, not how we shall please God, but how we shall conceal the prevailing dispositions of our hearts from those about us. A task this as difficult as it is mean: for whatever occupies our thoughts and affections, will, on various occasions, notwithstanding our utmost care, escape us. Looks, gestures, manner of speaking and acting, as well as words and deeds themselves, betray what is predominant within. Hence it is that we generally deceive ourselves in these matters. We often fancy our character to be unknown when it is well known: and if it were otherwise, all is naked and open to the eyes of him with whom we have to do. Of this we may be certain, that while our chief concern is to hide our sins from those about us, should we be summoned to give an account of our stewardship, it will appear that we *have sinned, and not repented of our deeds;* which, wherein it differs from going down to the grave *with our guilt upon our heads,* is difficult to say.

Sixthly, IF WE TAKE PLEASURE IN TALKING OF THE EVIL, OR IN DWELLING UPON IT IN OUR THOUGHTS, it is a certain sign of the same thing. True repentance works in a way of silent shame and self-abasement—*That thou mayest remember and be confounded, and never open thy mouth any more, because of thy shame, when I am pacified towards thee for all that thou hast done, saith the Lord God.*[1] When men can talk, and even write of their former wicked courses with lightness, it is a certain proof that whatever repentance they have had they do not *at present* repent of it; and though nothing be said or written, yet if such things occupy our thoughts, imaginations, and affections, it is much the same. A mind full of this must needs be *lacking* of those spiritual exercises, which render us that we shall neither be barren nor unfruitful in the knowledge of our Lord and Saviour Jesus Christ; and those that are such are fitly enough described as having *forgotten that they were purged from their old sins.*[2] If old sins are thought of with new delight, they are reacted and persisted in; and where this continues to be the case, the guilt of them must remain upon us, and may be found upon our heads when we go down to the grave.

Lastly, IF WE TRIFLE WITH TEMPTATION, OR BE NOT AFRAID OF PUTTING OURSELVES IN THE WAY OF IT, OR EVEN OF BEING LED INTO IT, we may be certain that we at present have not repented of our sin.—It is a saying almost grown into a proverb, He that is not afraid of temptation is not afraid of

1 Ezekiel 16:63.
2 2 Peter 1:5–9.

sin; and he that is not afraid of sin must needs be in danger of being destroyed by it. If, after having been repeatedly drawn into sin by associating in certain companies, or engaging in certain pursuits, we can nevertheless run into them again without fear, we cannot possibly have repented of our deeds. Nay more, though we should fear to plunge ourselves into temptation, yet if when providence brings us into such situations and companies, our hearts secretly rejoice in it, this is no less an evidence of our impenitent state than the other. True repentance will not only teach us to shun the way of evil, but to be averse to every avenue that leads to it. If, therefore, we either run into temptation, or are glad when we are led into it, we are beyond all doubt under the power of it.

Chapter 3

ON THE INJURIOUS AND DANGEROUS EFFECTS OF SIN LYING UPON THE CONSCIENCE UNLAMENTED

I t is a dangerous thing to fall into sin, whether secretly or openly, and the effects of it, sooner or later, will certainly be felt; but to continue in it is much more so. A very heavy threatening is denounced against God's open enemies for their *persisting* in sin: *God shall wound the head of his enemies, and the hairy scalp of such an one as* GOETH ON STILL *in his trespasses.*[1] But the same thing in persons who have known the way of righteousness, must be abundantly more offensive. *He that chastiseth the heathen, shall not He correct.*[2] There is a remedy at hand of God's providing; a *propitiation* for our sins; and it is declared, *If any man sin, we have an advocate with the Father, Jesus Christ the righteous.* But if instead of confessing our sins on the head of this propitiation, and imploring mercy in his name, we sink into hardness of heart, neglect prayer, shun the company of the faithful, and efface the remembrance of one sin only by the commission of another, what have we to expect?

I am aware that it is one of the devices of Satan, after having drawn a soul from God, and entangled him in the net of his

---

1 Psalm 68:21.
2 Psalm 94:10.

own corruptions, to persuade him that the prayer of faith in his circumstances would be presumption; and that it is much more modest and becoming for him to stand aloof both from God and his people. And if by faith were meant, what some would seem to understand by it, a working up ourselves into a persuasion that owing to the immutability of God all is safe and right, whatever be our spirit or conduct, it would be presumptuous enough: but genuine faith in Christ is never out of season. The greater our sin has been, the greater reason there is for us to confess it upon the head of the gospel sacrifice, and to plead for mercy in his name. We may not be able to go, considering ourselves as Christians but this affords no reason why we should not go as sinners.

The injury and danger of such a state of mind will appear from a consideration of the *effects* which it produces; and must continue to produce, if not healed by a return to God by Jesus Christ.

First, It will necessarily deprive us of all true enjoyment in religion, and by consequence, of all that preservation to the heart and mind which such enjoyment affords.—The principal sources of enjoyment to a Christian that walketh spiritually, are, communion with God and his people: but to him that is out of the way these streams are dried up: or, which is the same thing in effect to him, they are so impeded as not to reach him. Guilt, shame, darkness, and defilement have taken possession of the soul: love is quenched, hope clouded, joy fled, prayer restrained, and every other grace enervated. It becomes the holiness of God to frown upon us under such a state of mind, by withholding the light of his countenance; and if it were otherwise, we have no manner of desire after it. Such was the state of David after he had sinned, and before he had repented: the *joys of God's salvation* were far from him. The thirty-second and thirty-eighth Psalms appear to have been written, as has already been observed, after his recovery: but he there describes what was the state of his mind previous to it. There is much meaning in what he sets out with in the first of these psalms: *Blessed is he whose transgression is forgiven, and whose sin is covered—Blessed is the man to whom the Lord imputeth not iniquity, and in whose spirit there is no guile!*[1] He knew the contrary of this by bitter experience. Guilt and defilement had eaten up all his enjoyment. *When I kept silence*, saith he, *my bones waxed old, through my roaring all the day long: for day and night thy hand was heavy upon me: my moisture is turned into the drought of summer.*[2] It does not appear that he fully desisted from prayer; but there was none of that freedom in it which he was wont to enjoy. It was *roaring* rather than praying; and God is represented as disregarding it. In the thirty-eighth psalm he speaks of the *rebukes* of God's wrath, and the *chastening of his hot displeasure; of his arrows sticking fast in him, and his hand pressing him sore: of there being no soundness in his flesh because of his anger, nor rest in his bones because of his sin.*[3] There is one expression exceedingly appropriate: *My wounds stink and are corrupt, because of my foolishness.*[4] A wound may be dangerous at the time of its being received; but much more so if it be neglected till the humors of the body are drawn towards it. In this case it is hard to be healed; and the patient has not only to reflect on his heedlessness in first exposing himself to danger, but on his *foolishness* in so long neglecting the prescribed remedy. Such was the state

---

1 Psalm 32:1, 2.
2 Psalm 32:3, 4.
3 Psalm 38:1, 2, 3.
4 Psalm 38:5.

of his mind, till, as he informs us, he *acknowledged his trans-gressions, and was sorry for his sin.*[1]

And as there can be no communion with God, so neither can there be any *with his people.* If our sin be known, it must naturally have occasioned a reservedness, if not an exclusion from their society. Or if it be unknown, we shall be equally unable to enjoy communion with them. Guilt in our consciences will beget shame, and incline us rather to stand aloof than to come near them; or if we go into their company, it will prove a bar to freedom. There is something at first sight rather singular in the language of the apostle John; but upon close inspection, it will be found to be perfectly just: *If we walk in the light as he is in the light, we have fellowship one with another.*[2]

But if we are deprived of fellowship with God and his people, from what can we derive consolation? If we have only had a name to live, and been dead, the joy arising from vain hope may possibly be supplied by carnal pleasures. We may drown reflection by busying ourselves in worldly pursuits, mingling with worldly company, and in short, returning *like the dog to his vomit, and the sow that was washed to her wallowing in the mire:*[3] but if we have any true religion in us, we cannot do this; and then what is there under the sun that can yield relief!

Nor shall we be deprived merely of the enjoyments of religion, but of all that *preservation* to the soul which they afford. The *peace of God* is represented as that which *keeps* or fortifies *our hearts and minds.*[4] Without this the *heart* will be in continual danger of being seduced by the wiles, or sunk by

---

1 Psalm 38:18.

2 1 John 1:7.

3 2 Peter 2:22.

4 Philippians 4:7.

the pressures of this world; and the *mind* of being drawn aside from the simplicity of the gospel.

Secondly, IT WILL RENDER US USELESS IN OUR GENERATION.—The great end of existence with a good man, is to live to him who died for us and rose again. If God bless us, it is that like Abraham we may be blessings to others. Christians are said to be the salt of the earth, and the light of the world; but while we are in the state above described, we are as *salt that has lost its savor*, which is *good for nothing;* or as a light that is hid under a vessel. Of what use with respect to religion are we in our families, while this is the case? Neither servants nor children think well of religion from any thing they see in us; and when we go into the world, and mingle among mankind in our dealings, in whose conscience does our conversation or behavior plant conviction? Where is the man, who, on leaving our company, has been compelled by it to acknowledge the reality of religion? Or if we occupy a station in the church of God (and this character may belong to a minister no less than to another man) we shall do little or no good in it; but be as *vessels in which the Lord taketh no pleasure.* There is a threatening directed against vain pastors, which ought to make a minister tremble. *Woe to the idol shepherd, that leaveth the flock! The sword shall be upon his arm, and upon his right eye: his arm shall be clean dried up, and his right eye shall be utterly darkened.*[1] Perhaps one of the greatest temptations to backsliding in ministers may lie in this way: being selected from their brethren, and chosen to the office of public instructors, they are in danger of indulging in self-valuation. A man may labor night and day in his study, and all to get accomplished, that he may shine before the people. When this is the case, the preacher is his own *idol*, and it may be, that of the people. He feels little or no regard

1 Zechariah 11:17.

to the charge which he has undertaken, but is ready to desert it whenever a difficulty arises, or any opportunity offers of improving his circumstances. The consequence is, the sword of the Lord is upon *his arm*—he does no manner of execution in his work; and upon his *right eye*—whatever proficiency he may make in science, or polite accomplishments, he has but little, if any, spiritual understanding in the things of God. This character may respect ungodly preachers, such to whom the Jewish nation were given up for their rejection of Christ; but there is no sin committed by the most ungodly man, of which the most godly is not in danger.

Thirdly, WE SHALL NOT ONLY BE USELESS, BUT INJURIOUS TO THE CAUSE OF CHRIST.—Indeed it is impossible to stand neuter in this cause. If we do no good, we shall do harm; not only as cumberers of the ground, occupying that place in society which might be better filled by others, but as giving a false representation of religion, and diffusing a savor of death among mankind. If our domestics infer nothing favorable to religion from our conduct in the family, they will infer something unfavorable; and if there be but little good to be seen in our example, it is well if there be not much evil; and this will surely be imitated. Who can calculate what influence the treachery, unchastity, and murder committed by David, had upon his family? We know that each was acted over again by Ammon and Absalom. And thus many a parent has seen his own sins repeated in his posterity; and perhaps, if he had lived longer might have seen them multiplied still more to his shame and confusion.

The servants of God are called to bear testimony for him: *Ye are my witnesses, saith the Lord of Hosts.*[1] This is not done merely by words, but by deeds. There is a way of bearing

1 Isaiah 44:8.

witness to the reality and importance of religion by a zealous perseverance in it, to its dignity by our firmness, to its happy influence by contentedness and cheerfulness, and to its purity by being holy in all manner of conversation: and this is a kind of testimony which is more regarded than any other. Men in common form their judgments of religion more by what they see in the professors of it, than by the profession itself. Hence it was that David by his *deed* is said to have *given great occasion to the enemies of the Lord to blaspheme.*[1] They were not contented with reproaching him, but must speak against God and religion on his account. In this view he considered his sin when he was brought to repentance for it. *Against* THEE, THEE *only have I sinned, and done this evil in thy sight.*[2]—*Do good in thy good pleasure unto Zion: build thou the walls of Jerusalem.*[3] If his sin had not greatly dishonored God's name, and, as it were, broken down the walls of Zion, such language would not have appeared among his lamentations. Things operate much the same to this day. Whatever evil is done by a professor, it is ascribed to his religion. In this view we may justly consider our unchristian conduct as bearing false witness of God; for it is giving false representations of his gospel and government to the world. A grasping selfish spirit is saying to those around us, that, after all which we have professed of living by faith in a portion beyond death, the present world is the best, and therefore we are for making sure of that, and running all hazards as to the other. In like manner a cruel and revengeful disposition towards those who have offended us, is saying, that Christianity, after all its professions of meekness and forgiveness of injuries, renders its adherents no better than others.

1 2 Samuel 12:14.
2 Psalm 51:4.
3 Psalm 51:18.

And when a Christian professor is detected of having privately indulged in the lusts of the flesh, the conclusion that is drawn from it is, that there is nothing in religion but outside appearance, and that religious people are the same as others in secret. It is impossible to say how much such conduct operates to the hardening of men in sin, to the quenching of their convictions, to the weakening of the hands of God's servants, and to the stumbling of persons who are inquiring the way to Zion.

These things, if we be mere professors, may have but little effect upon us. We may not care for God's being dishonored, provided we do but get pardoned at last: but if there be any true religion about us, it will be otherwise. An ingenuous mind will feel more for the dishonor which he has done to Christ, and injury to his fellow creatures, than for the reproach which he has brought upon himself.

Fourthly, WE ARE IN THE UTMOST DANGER OF FALLING INTO FUTURE TEMPTATIONS, AND SO OF SINKING DEEPER, AND FALLING FARTHER FROM GOD.—So long as sin remains upon the conscience unlamented, it is like poison in the constitution: it will be certain to operate; and that in a way that shall go on more and more to kill all holy resolution, to harden the heart, and to defile the imaginations and desires. *Whoredom and wine, and new wine, take away the heart.*[1] It is from sad experience of the defiling nature of past sin, that David when he came to himself prayed as he did; *Create in me a* CLEAN HEART, *O God, and renew a right spirit within me.*[2]

A mind thus enfeebled, stupified, and defiled, must needs be in a very unfit condition to resist new temptations. The inhabitants of a besieged city, who are weakened by famine and disease, and discouraged by a number of disaffected persons

1 Hosea 4:11.
2 Psalm 51:10.

within their walls, have no heart to resist, but stand ready to listen to the first proposals of the besiegers.

And in proportion as we are disabled for resistance it may be expected that the tempter will renew his attempts upon us. If Satan have any influence on the human mind, it may be supposed that he acts with design, and knows how to avail himself of the most favorable seasons to effect his purpose. And this we find to be true by experience. In proportion as we have yielded to temptation, it will rise in its demands; solicitations, greater in number and in force, will ply our minds. As a resistance of the devil will be followed by his *fleeing from us*, so, on the contrary, a non-resistance of him will be followed by renewed and stronger attempts upon us. One sin makes way for another, and renders us less able to resist, or to return to God by repentance. When once the thief has gained admission into our habitation, he will bid us defiance. *Innumerable evils will compass us about, and our iniquities take hold upon us, so that we shall not be able to look up: they will be more than the hairs of our heads; therefore our hearts will fail us.*[1] Sampson first yielded to his sensual desires; after this, to the entreaties of his Delilah, who in proportion as she saw him pliant to her wishes, increased in her assiduousness, till at length he lost his hair, his liberty, his eyes, and his life.

If we be mere professors, these considerations may effect us but little: we shall continue the willing slaves of our own corruptions, hoping, it may be, nevertheless, that we shall sometime be brought back again, till at some unexpected hour we are taken out of the world. But if there be any good thing in us towards the Lord God of Israel, this part of the subject alarms us: for of all the methods which God takes to punish sin, there is none more awful and more dreaded by a good

1 Psalm 40:12.

man, than that of being *given up to sin*.

Fifthly, SO LONG AS SIN REMAINS UPON THE CONSCIENCE UNLAMENTED, WE ARE IN DANGER OF ETERNAL DAMNATION.—It may be thought by some that such language is inconsistent with the final perseverance of believers: but it is manifest that our Lord did not so teach the doctrine of perseverance as to render cautions of this nature unnecessary. He did not scruple to declare, even to his own disciples, that, "Whosoever should say to his brother, thou fool, should be in danger of hell-fire.—That if they forgave not men their trespasses, neither would God forgive theirs—and if a right hand, or a right eye, caused them to offend, it must be cut off, or plucked out, and that lest the whole body should be cast into hell."[1]

The object at which sin aims, whether in believers or unbelievers, is *death, eternal death;* and to this it hath a natural and direct tendency. The apostle James in a very affecting manner describes its process. "Let no man say when he is tempted, I am tempted of God: for God cannot be tempted with evil, neither tempteth he any man: but every man is tempted when he is drawn away of his own lust and enticed. Then when lust hath conceived, it bringeth forth sin, and sin, when it is finished bringeth forth death."[2] If it does not in all cases come to this issue, it is not because of its being different as to its nature or tendency in some persons from what it is in others, but because a timely stop is put to its operations. Only let it go on without repentance till it has *finished* its work, and eternal death will be the issue.

Whatever we are, so long as sin lies unlamented upon the conscience, we can have no scriptural foundation to conclude

---

1 Matthew 5.
2 James 1:13–15.

that we are Christians. No real Christian, it is true, will prove an apostate; yet while we are under the influence of sin, we are moving in the direction which leads to apostasy. If we are contented with a relapsed state of mind, what grounds can we have to conclude that it is not our element, or that we have ever been the subjects of true religion? If the waters continue to be naught, it is a sign that the spring has not been healed. There is no reason to think that Judas himself laid his accounts with such an issue as things actually came to. During the ministry of our Lord, while he kept the bag, and sometimes made free with its contents, it is probable he nevertheless reckoned himself a good man. He saw many failings in his fellow-disciples, and in all other good men; and he might think this to be his. When he had covenanted with the chief priests, it does not appear that he expected his master would be eventually taken and crucified. When they were about to lay hands on him, he had often passed through the midst of them and went his way; and he might suppose that it would be so again. *When therefore he saw that he was condemned*, he was thrown into a state of terrible amazement, and in the issue went and *hanged himself.* Such was the process of an apostate; and such his end. Surely it behoves us to take heed how we trifle with those things, the end of which is death?

Chapter 4

ON THE MEANS OF RECOVERY

Were it not for the hopes of being instrumental in saving some from the error of their way, and of inducing others to a greater degree of watchfulness, I should not have written the preceding pages. It can afford no satisfaction to expose the evil conduct of a fellow-sinner, or to trace its dangerous effects, unless it be with a view to his salvation or preservation.

It is natural for those who have fallen into sin, unless they be given up to a rejection of all religion, to wish, on some consideration, to be restored. A backsliding state is far from being agreeable. Hence it is that many have prematurely grasped at the promise of forgiveness, and said to their souls, *Peace, peace, when there was no peace*. It is desirable that we be recovered from our backslidings; but it is not desirable that we should think ourselves recovered when we are not so.

As there are many ways by which a convinced sinner seeks peace to his soul, without being able to find it, so it is with a backslider. Self-righteous attempts to mortify sin, and gain peace with God, are not confined to the first period of religious concern. Having through the power of alarm desisted from the open practice of sin, many have labored to derive comfort from this consideration, without confessing their sin on the head, as it were, of the gospel sacrifice. Their sins may be said rather to have been *worn* away from their remembrance, by length of time, than *washed* away by the blood of the cross. But this is not recovery; the hurt, if healed, is healed slightly; and may be expected to break out again. The same way in which, if we be true Christians, we first found rest to our souls must be pursued in order to re-recover it; namely, by *repentance towards God, and faith towards our Lord Jesus Christ.* This is the way to which the scriptures uniformly direct us. "My little children, these things I write unto you, that ye sin not. And if any man sin, we have an advocate with the Father, Jesus Christ the righteous."[1]—"If we confess our sins, he is faithful and just to forgive us our sins, and to cleanse us from all unrighteousness."[2] This was the way in which David was recovered. He confessed his sin with deep contrition, pleading to be purged *with hyssop, that he might be clean and washed that he might be whiter than snow.*[3] By this language he could not mean that his sin should be purged away by anything pertaining to the ceremonial law, for that law made no provision for the pardon of his crimes: he must therefore intend that which the sprinkling of the unclean with a bunch of hyssop, dipped in the water of purification, was designed to prefigure; which, as we are taught in the New Testament, was the *purging of the conscience, by the sprinkling of the blood of Jesus.*[4]

This is the only way in which it is possible to find rest to our souls. As there is no other name given under heaven, or among men, by which we can be saved, so neither is there any

---

1 1 John 2:1.

2 1 John 1:9.

3 Psalm 51:7.

4 Hebrews 9:14–28.

other by which we can be restored. Whatever be the nature of our backsliding from God, this must be the remedy. If it be a *relinquishment of evangelical principles*, we must return to the way, even the highway whither we went. Paul *travailed in birth* for the recovery of the Galatians; and in what did he expect it to consist? In *Christ being formed in them*. He also strove to bring back the Hebrews; and all his labors were directed to the same point, His epistle to them is full of *Christ*, and of warnings and cautions against neglecting and rejecting him. If any man have been perplexed concerning the deity or atonement of Christ, let him humbly and carefully read that epistle: and if his heart be right with God, it will do him good. If our departure from God have issued in *some gross immorality,* or in *the love of the world*, or in *conformity to it*, the remedy must be the same. It is by this medium, if at all, that the world will be crucified unto us, and we unto the world. If we have no heart to repent, and return to God by Jesus Christ, we are yet in our sins, and may expect to reap the fruits of them. The scriptures give no counsel to anything short of this. They are not wanting, however, in directions that may lead to it, and considerations that may induce it. What these are I shall now proceed to inquire.

In general, I may observe, The scriptures assure us of the *exceeding great and tender mercy of God, and of his willingness to forgive all those who return to him in the name of his Son.*—It is necessary that we be well persuaded of this truth, lest, instead of applying as supplicants, we sink into despair. If an awakened sinner under his first religious concern be in danger of this species of despondency, a backslider is still more so. His transgressions are much more heinous in their circumstances than those of the other, having been committed under greater light, and against greater goodness: and when to this is added the treatment which his conduct must necessarily draw upon him from his religious connections, he may be tempted to relinquish all hopes of recovery, and to consider himself as an outcast of both God and man. Unhappy man! Thy breach may be *great like the sea*, and the language of an awakened conscience may suggest, *Who can heal me?* Yet do not despair. *Hear what God the Lord will speak. He will speak peace unto his people, and to his saints: but let them not turn again to folly.* Hear what he speaks to the backsliding Israelites, reduced by their sins to the most deplorable state of guilt and wretchedness. "The Lord shall scatter you among the nations, and ye shall be left few among the heathen, whither the Lord shall lead you. And there ye shall serve gods, the works of men's hands; but if from *thence* thou shalt seek the Lord thy God, thou shalt find him, if thou seek him with all thy heart and with all thy soul: when thou art in tribulation, and all these things are come up on thee, if thou turn to the Lord thy God, and shalt be obedient unto his voice, (for the Lord thy God is a merciful God) he will not forsake thee, nor forget the covenant of thy fathers which he sware unto them."[1] The pardoning mercy of God towards those who return to him by Jesus Christ is not limited by such measures as are framed by creatures in their treatment of one another, or by such expectations as, on this account, they are apt to form. There are circumstances which may render it almost impossible for forgiveness to be exercised among men; and therefore men are ready to think it must be so with respect to God. But *with the Lord there is mercy, and with him there is plenteous redemption.* He will not only pardon, but pardon *abundantly:*[2] for his thoughts are not as our thoughts, nor his ways as our ways. For as the heavens are

1 Deuteronomy 4:27–31.
2 Psalm 130:7, 8.

higher than the earth, so are his ways higher than our ways, and his thoughts than our thoughts.[1]—"The blood of Jesus Christ his Son cleanseth us from *all sin*."[2]—"If we confess our sins, he is faithful and just to forgive us our sins, and to cleanse us from *all unrighteousness*."[3] The threatenings against the *unpardonable sin* itself do not affect the truth of these merciful declarations; for that sin is all along described as excluding *repentance* as well as forgiveness.[4] The person is supposed to be given up to hardness of heart. If therefore we *confess* our sin with contrition, we may be certain it is not unpardonable, and that we shall obtain mercy through the blood of the cross.

But the great question is, *How we shall repent of our sins, and return to God by Jesus Christ?* Undoubtedly it is much easier to get out of the way than to get in again; to lose the peace of our minds than to recover it. Sin is of a hardening nature; and the farther we have proceeded in it, the more inextricable are its chains. But however this be, we either do desire to return, or we do not. If *not*, it will be in vain to address any directions to us. It is right indeed for the servants of Christ to point them out, whether we will hear or whether we will forbear; and there leave them: but as to any hope of our recovery, while such is the state of our minds, there can be none. If we can think of our sin without grief, and of the cross of Christ without any meltings of spirit, there is great reason to fear that our *hearts are not right in the sight of God:* but that we are yet in the *gall of bitterness, and the bonds of iniquity*. If, on the other hand, we *do* desire to return; if, like Israel in the days of Samuel, we *lament after the Lord*, we shall readily hearken to

---

1 Isaiah 55:7–9.

2 1 John 1:7.

3 1 John 1:9.

4 Hebrews 6:6; 1 John 1:7–8.

every direction given us in his word.

If my reader, supposing him to have backslidden from God, be in such a state of mind, it is with a mixture of hope and tenderness that I attempt to point out to him the means of recovery. Or should it even be otherwise, I will nevertheless endeavor to show him the good and the right way, that at least I may deliver my own soul.

First, Embrace every possible season of retirement for reading the Holy Scriptures, especially those parts which are suited to thy case, and accompany it with prayer.— God's Word hid in the heart, is not only a preservative against sin, but a restorative from it. It both wounds and heals: if it rebukes, it is with the faithfulness of a friend: or if it consoles, its consolations carry in them an implication, which, if properly understood, will melt us into repentance.

Read especially those parts of Scripture which are *addressed to persons in your situation;* as the second chapter of Jeremiah: or which express the desires of a returning sinner; as the twenty-fifth, thirty-second, thirty-eighth, fifty-first, and hundred-and-thirtieth psalms. You may not be able to adopt all this language as your own: but it may be useful nevertheless. To read the genuine expressions of a contrite heart, may produce at least a conviction of the disparity between the frame of mind possessed by the writer and yourself: and such a conviction may be accompanied with a sensation of shame and grief.

It is also of importance that you read the Scriptures *by yourself.* To read a portion of them in your families is right, and ought not to be neglected: but there is a wide difference, as to personal advantage, between this and reading them alone. Your mind may then be more at liberty for reflection; you can read, and pause, and think, and apply the subject to your case.

It is of still greater importance to *unite prayer with it.*

Reading the Word of God and prayer, are duties which mutually assist each other; the one furnisheth us with confessions, pleas and arguments, while the other promotes solemnity and spirituality of mind, which goes farther towards understanding the Scriptures, than a library of expositions.

It was in one of these seasons of retirement that David put up this petition, "I have gone astray like a lost sheep: seek thy servant; for I do not forget thy commandments."[1] He seems to have had in his thoughts the condition of a poor wandering sheep, that had left the flock, and the rich pastures whither it was wont to be led; ranging rather like a native of the woods, than one which had been led, and fed, and protected by its owner. Bewildered by its own wanderings, entangled in the thorns and briars of the wilderness, and exposed to beasts of prey, it feels its forlorn condition, and bleats after the shepherd and the flock! Is there nothing in this that may suit thy case? Yes, thou art the man! Thou hast gone astray like a lost sheep, got entangled in thine own corruptions, and knowest not how to find the way back: yet it may be thou hast not *forgotten his commandments*, not utterly lost the savor of those happy days when walking in them. Let thy prayer then be directed like that of the Psalmist, to the good shepherd of the sheep, *Seek thy servant!*

Prayer is a kind of religious exercise which is necessary to accompany all others. "In everything by prayer and supplication, with thanksgiving, let your requests be made known unto God."[2] Solemn approaches unto God are adapted to impress the mind with a sense of sin, and to inspire us with self-abhorrence on account of it. It was by a view of the holiness of God that Isaiah felt himself to be *a man of unclean lips;* and by

1 Psalm 119:176.
2 Philippians 4:6.

conversing with him that Job was brought to *abhor himself and repent in dust and ashes*. The very exercise of prayer carries in it an implication that *our help must come from above;* a truth which in all cases it is highly necessary for us to know, and with which, in this case especially, we cannot be too deeply impressed. We easily get out of the way; but if ever we return to it, it must be by his influence who *restoreth our souls, and leadeth us in the paths of righteousness, for his name sake.*[1]

To tell a person who is out of the way, that he has no help of himself, and that if ever he get in again it must be by the restoring grace of God, may seem to some people paradoxical and disheartening: but it is a truth, and a truth which if properly understood and felt, would go farther towards our recovery than we at first may apprehend. Paul found that *when he was weak then was he strong;* and many others have found the same. The more we are emptied of self-sufficiency, the more sensibly shall we feel our dependence, and the more importunately implore that the Lord would save us as it were from ourselves, and restore us *for his name sake.*

This was the way in which we at first found rest for our souls, and this must be the way in which we recover it. An awakened sinner frequently labors hard after peace, without being able to obtain it. Wherefore? "Because he seeks it not by faith, but as it were by the works of the law, stumbling at the stumbling-stone."[2] In all his labors there is a large portion of self-righteous hope, or an idea that God will pity him on account of his painful endeavors to please him. But this is like bad flesh in a wound, which must be eaten out before it can be healed. If ever he obtain peace, it must be by utterly despairing of all help from himself, and falling, as a sinner entirely lost,

---

1 Psalm 23:3.
2 Romans 9:32.

into the arms of sovereign mercy. This is *walking in the good old way,* which brings *rest to the soul:* and the same sense of our insufficiency which is necessary to find rest in the first instance, is equally necessary to find it in all that follow.

We may pray from year to year, and all without effect. It is only *the prayer of faith* that succeeds; the distinguishing characteristic of which is, under a sense of there being no help in us, to lay hold of the mercy and faithfulness of God, as revealed in the gospel. David for a time *groaned,* and even *roared, by reason of the disquietness of his heart:* but he obtained no relief from this. On the contrary, he sunk deeper and deeper into despondency. At length he betook him to another *manner* of praying. *Out of the* DEPTHS CRIED I UNTO THEE: *and thou heardest my voice!* We find him here pleading the exceeding *greatness of God's mercy, and the plenteousness of his redemption.*[1] Here he found rest for his soul!—Jonah also for a time was in much the same state. With a conscience so far awakened as to deprive him of all enjoyment, he retired to the bottom of the ship; and wearied with the load of his guilt, slept away his time. Even the horrors of a tempest did not awaken him. At length being roused, and reproved by heathens, and marked out by lot as the guilty person, he confesses who he is, and what he had done, and advises them to cast him into the sea. Humanity struggles for a time with the elements, but in vain; he must be cast away. Think what a state of mind he must at this time have possessed! He is thrown into the deep, is swallowed by a fish, and retains his reason even in that situation; but no light shines upon his soul. Conceiving himself to be on the point of expiring, his heart sighed within him, *I am cast out of thy sight!* But ere the thought had well passed his mind, another struck him—*Yet will I look again towards thy*

1 Psalm 38 and 130.

holy temple![1] He looked, and was lightened: *Out of the belly of hell cried I unto thee, and thou heardest my voice!*[2]

Secondly, REFLECT ON THE AGGRAVATING CIRCUMSTANCES OF THINE OFFENSES, or on those things which render it *an evil and bitter thing* to have departed from the living God, and to have sinned against him in the manner thou hast done.—Every return to God begins with reflection. "I thought on my ways, and turned my feet unto thy testimonies."[3]—"Commune with thine own heart upon thy bed, and be still."[4] "If the God against whom I have sinned had been like the idols of this world, I might have been justified in departing from him but I have acted the part of the backsliding Israelites, who were the only people who had a God worth cleaving to, and yet were the only people distinguished by their fickleness. The world cleave close enough to their gods, which yet are no gods: but I have committed those two evils at which the heavens are astonished. I have forsaken the fountain of living waters, and hewed to myself cisterns, broken cisterns that can hold no water! If the service of the Lord had been a heavy yoke, and if the way of his commandments had been an unfruitful and miserable path, I might have some plea for deserting it: but what have I gained except guilt, and shame, and wretchedness, by leaving him? Was he a barren wilderness to me, or a land of darkness? How can I answer his tender, yet cutting expostulations—'O my people, what have I done unto thee: wherein have I wearied thee? Testify against me!'[5]

"If I had been born and educated a benighted pagan, a deluded Mohammedan, or a superstitious papist: if the oracles

1 Jonah 2:4.
2 Jonah 2:2.
3 Psalm 119:59.
4 Psalm 4:4.
5 Micah 6:3.

of God had been withheld from me; or if I had lived all my days in a state of ignorance and insensibility, like multitudes in my native country, the sins that I have committed had been little in comparison of what they now are. I have verged near to the unpardonable sin. It is against *light* and *love* that I have offended. He has been as a husband unto me: but I have forsaken him, and have gone after other lovers. Yet he still invites me to return. And what hindereth? I am not straitened in him, but in my own bowels. Lord save me from myself! *Surely I will return to my first husband, for then was it better with me than now.*"

Thirdly, REFLECT ON THE GOODNESS OF GOD IN HAVING HITHERTO BORNE WITH THEE, and prevented thy sins from fully operating according to their native tendency.—It is a common observation that one sin leads on to another. Of this history and experience furnish many tragic examples. The sauntering indolence of David occasioned his adultery. Adultery when committed must be concealed, and this leads to treachery and intrigue. When these fail, recourse is had to murder. And when the murder is effected, to carry on the concealment the event must be attributed to providence— *The sword devoureth one as well as another!*[1] The connection between uncleanness and blood is strongly marked in the history of human crimes. A large proportion of those who have been publicly executed for the one, were induced to perpetrate the horrid deed as a covert to the other. And hast thou been tampering with these vices; playing at the hole of the cockatrice den? How is it that death and hell have not ere now swallowed thee up? Behold that wretch who went but yesterday to suffer the just vengeance of his country, for having murdered the object whom he had first seduced; and see

1 2 Samuel 11:25.

what thou mightest have been! Is it not owing to singular mercy that thy sins have been restrained from their wonted and deadly issues?

It may be, some who have been companions, or at least contemporaries, with thee in the first stages of sin, have meanwhile been suffered to make more rapid progress. Their follies have ended in infamy, while thine have been restrained, and comparatively hid. And it is possible, while the public voice has been raised against them, thou hast joined it.

"And thinkest thou this, O man, that judgest them which do such things, and doest the same, that thou shalt escape the judgment of God? Or despisest thou the riches of his goodness, and forbearance, and long-suffering, not knowing that the goodness of God leadeth thee to repentance?"[1] If the recollection of such things leadeth thee not to repentance, it is a dark sign of "a hard and impenitent heart treasuring up to itself wrath against the day of wrath, and revelation of the righteous judgment of God."

Fourthly, REFLECT ON THE STATE AND EXERCISES OF THY MIND IN FORMER TIMES.—This was the counsel of the apostle to the Hebrews, who, disheartened by persecution, were half inclined to go back again to Judaism: "Call to remembrance the former days, in which, after that ye were illuminated, ye endured a great fight of afflictions."[2] This was the counsel of our Lord himself, to the churches of Ephesus and Sardis: "Remember from whence thou art fallen, and repent"[3]— "remember how thou hast received and heard, and hold fast, and repent."[4] Ask thine own soul, "Are there no seasons of

1 Romans 2:3, 4.
2 Hebrews 10:32.
3 Revelation 2:5.
4 Revelation 3:3.

tenderness in my life which it would be for my profit to recall
to mind? I have professed repentance towards God, and faith
towards our Lord Jesus Christ: and was it only a profession?
Was there not a time when my sins were more bitter to me
than death, and more dreaded than hell? How is it that I have
turned again to folly? Has sin changed its nature, or become
less odious? Rather is not the change in me? Was there not
a time when the Word of the Lord was precious to my soul;
when my Sabbaths were my happiest days, and godly people
my chosen companions? Whence this lamentable change?
Is Christ or the gospel less precious than heretofore? I once
thought that if I might but be found in him, and live for ever
with him and those that love him, I should not care what I
lost or suffered in the present world. And was I all this time
deceiving myself? Were my repentance, and faith, and hope,
and love, and joy, all counterfeit? I endured reproaches and
losses, as I supposed, for his name, sake; and is it all *in vain?*
Must I at last be separated for ever from him, and have my portion with unbelievers? 'O Lord, have mercy upon me a most
wretched caitiff and miserable sinner! I have offended both
against heaven and earth more than my tongue can express!
Whither then may I go, or whither shall I flee? To heaven I
may be ashamed to lift up mine eyes, and on earth I find no
place of refuge, or succor. To THEE, therefore, O Lord, do I
run: TO THEE do I humble myself. O Lord, my God, my sins
are great: but yet have mercy upon me, for thy great mercy.
The great mystery, that God became man, was not wrought
for small or few offenses. Thou didst not give thy Son unto
death for little sins only: but for all the greatest sins of the
world, so that the sinner returns to thee with his whole heart,
as I do here at this present. Wherefore have mercy on me, O
God, whose property is always to have mercy. Have mercy

upon me, O Lord, for thy great mercy. O Lord, I crave nothing for my own merits, but for thy name sake, that it might be
hallowed thereby, and for thy dear Son Jesus Christ's sake.'"[1]

This part of our Lord's counsel would apply not only to
those who have fallen into gross immoralities, but to such
as have deserted *the principles of the gospel*. It was asked the
Galatians, through what medium it was that they first *received
the Spirit; by the works of the law, or by the hearing of faith?*[2]
This question proceeds upon the principle of that being the
true doctrine which is productive of the best effects; and by
the manner in which it is introduced, *This* ONLY *would I
learn of you*, it is intimated that the solution is of *itself* suffi-
cient to determine what the true doctrine is. And what are the
effects produced by a relinquishment of the doctrines usually
denominated evangelical? Nay, I might say, by only a hesita-
tion concerning them? I appeal to those who have made the
trial. Have you the same joy and peace in believing in your
present principles, as you had in your former ones? Can you,
or do you go to a throne of grace with the same holy freedom
as heretofore? Do you feel an equal concern for the salvation
of your poor ungodly neighbors? Rather is not the far greater
part of your zeal consumed in laboring to make proselytes of
serious Christians to your new way of thinking? Does the society of those who are like minded with yourself, afford that
inward satisfaction which you once enjoyed in the fellowship
of those whom you are now taught to pity as enthusiasts?

---

1 That which is included in inverted commas is a part of the prayer of
Archbishop CRANMER, who, through fear of man, had denied his faith,
but was notwithstanding burned to death. When brought to execution,
which was at Oxford, on March 21, 1556, he uttered the above prayer;
and on the flames approaching him, first thrust into the fire the hand with
which he had signed his recantation.

2 Galatians 3:2.

If while professing those things you are strangers to them, you may answer these questions in the affirmative: but if otherwise, you could not "Remember from whence you are fallen, and repent!" Remember how you have received and heard, and hold fast, and repent!

Fifthly, SET APART SPECIAL TIMES TO HUMBLE YOURSELF BEFORE GOD BY FASTING AND PRAYER.—Extraordinary cases require the use of extraordinary means. When a great army was coming against Jehoshaphat, it is said, *he feared, and* SET HIMSELF *to seek the Lord, and proclaimed a fast throughout all Judah.*[1] But the loss of a soul is of more account to you than the temporal overthrow of a country was to him. When Judah for its backslidings was under the frowns of God in Babylon, and had been so for about seventy years, Daniel says, I SET MY FACE *unto the Lord God, to seek by prayer and supplication, with fasting and sackcloth and ashes.*[2] The apostle Paul plainly intimates that there are times wherein we are required to *give ourselves to fasting and prayer.*[3] And surely there can be no times in which these means are more necessary than when we have got out of the way, and desire to recover it. There is much meaning in the words, *He* SET HIMSELF *to seek the Lord, and I* SET MY FACE *unto the Lord God.* They denote something more than the extraordinary exercises of prayer; even a special fixedness of the thoughts, purposes, and desires, to particular objects: and God has usually honored those extraordinary approaches to him, when influenced by a pure motive, with success. It is true, we may attend to duty in a superstitious, or self-righteous spirit; resting in it as an end, instead of using it as a means: but this is not *setting our face unto the Lord God,*

---

1 2 Chronicles 20:3.
2 Daniel 9:3.
3 1 Corinthians 7:5.

or seeking him. A day devoted to God in humiliation, fasting and prayer, occasionally occupied with reading suitable parts of the Holy Scriptures, may, by the blessing of the Holy Spirit, contribute more to the subduing of sin, and the recovery of a right mind, than years spent in a sort of half-hearted exercises.

Sixthly, To PRAYER IT IS NECESSARY TO ADD WATCHFUL-NESS.—Our Lord unites these together as an antidote against temptation. It has sometimes been one of the devices of Satan, after a backslider has been drawing near to God, and strongly soliciting for mercy; yea, after a time has been set apart for this purpose, to ply him afresh with some powerful tempta-tion: and while his mind has been unsuspicious, and it may be thinking itself to be somewhat secure on account of having so lately been engaged in earnest devotion, he has been sur-prised, and overcome! The consequence, as might be expected has been, a future neglect of prayer, under the idea that it must have been mere hypocrisy before, and would now be adding sin to sin. Instead of depending upon spiritual frames for pres-ervation, and especially when they are over, perhaps we ought to expect that our comforts should be succeeded by conflicts. We know it was so in several cases recorded in the Scriptures. Immediately after drinking at the smitten rock at Rephidim, Israel was called to fight with Amalek. Paul's thorn in the flesh succeeded to extraordinary revelations. Our Lord himself went up from Jordan into the wilderness to be tempted of the devil.

Seventhly, IN YOUR APPROACHES TO THE SAVIOUR, LET IT BE UNDER THE CHARACTER IN WHICH YOU FIRST APPLIED TO HIM FOR MERCY, THAT OF A SINNER.—If you attempt to approach the throne of grace as a good man who has backslid-den from God, you may find it impossible to support that character. The reality of your conversion may be doubtful, not only in your apprehension, but in itself. Your approach, therefore, must not be as one that *is washed, and needeth not, save to wash his feet:* but as one who is defiled throughout, *whose hands and head,* and every part needs to be cleansed. Do not employ yourself in raking over the rubbish of your past life in search of evidence that your are a Christian. You will not be able in your present state of mind to decide that question: nor would it be of any service to you if you could decide it. One thing is certain; you are *a sinner,* a poor miserable perishing sinner: the door of mercy is open; and you are welcome to enter it. Let your past character then have been what it may, and let your conversion be ever so doubtful, if you can *from this time* relinquish all for Christ eternal life is before you.

The Laodiceans, who, though composing a Christian church, were doubtful characters, are counselled to deal with Christ in the same manner as *sinners* deal with him, for *riches,* for *righteousness,* and for heavenly *wisdom.*

Lastly, IN ALL YOUR SUPPLICATIONS, BE CONTENTED WITH NOTHING SHORT OF A COMPLETE RECOVERY.—It is possible you may obtain so much ascendency over your evil propensities that they may seem to be slain before you; or at least, that you are in no particular danger of yielding to them any more; and yet you may not have recovered that holy rest in God, that sweet peace which arises from confessing our sins upon the head of the gospel sacrifice. But while this is the case there is no security against their revival. The first temptation by which you are assaulted may afford lamentable proof that they are yet alive. Nothing will serve as a preservative against the risings of evil propensities short of *walking with God.* There is much important truth in that declaration of the apostle, *This I say then, walk in the spirit, and ye shall not fulfil the lusts of the flesh.*[1] Sin is not to be opposed so much directly as indirectly:

1 Galatians 5:16.

not by mere resistance, but by opposing other principles to it. It is not by contending with the fire, especially with combustible materials about us, that we should be able to quench it; but by dealing plentifully with the opposite element. The pleasures of sense will not be effectually subdued by foregoing all enjoyment; but by imbibing other pleasures, the relish of which shall deaden the heart to what is opposite. It was thus that the apostle became *dead to the world by the cross of Christ*. Do not therefore reckon thyself restored till thou hast recovered communion with God. David, though the subject of deep contrition, yet was not contented without gaining this important point. Till then the poison would still at times be rankling in his imagination. Hence arose the following petitions—*Create in me a clean heart, O God, and renew a right spirit within me. Cast me not away from thy presence; and take not thy Holy Spirit from me. Restore unto me the joy of thy salvation; and uphold me with thy free Spirit.*[1] Make these petitions thy own: and if God grant the thing that thine heart desireth, go and sin no more, lest a worse thing come upon thee!

---

1 Psalm 51:10–12.

Made in the USA
Middletown, DE
24 October 2023